god

A Simple Book of Spirituality

god

A Simple Book of Spirituality

Ben HaYim

(Parenthesis Press)
Berkeley, California

www.ParenthesisPress.com
www.godisgoodness.com

FIRST PAPERBACK EDITION

Cover design by Ben HaYim and produced by
Lightbourne

This book is printed on acid free, recycled paper

HaYim, Ben.
    God : a simple book of spirituality / Ben
    HaYim. -- 1st ed.
        p. cm.
        Title appears on title page in all lower-case letters
        LCCN: 99-75065
        ISBN: 0-9674079-6-6

    1. God. 2. Spiritual life.   I. Title.

BL205.H39 2000   211
                              QBI99-1375

For my parents
Marian and Jack
who each in their own way
showed me the meaning
of goodness

Contents

Acknowledgments

I am very grateful to the countless people who have knowingly or unknowingly contributed to this book. Great sages in history and righteous souls still walking the earth have inspired me with their writing, ideas, and action. Some who played a role are cherished friends while others are people I briefly encountered and never saw again. From some, I gained insights through comments or conversation. From others I received encouragement to continue.

I especially want to thank those who played a direct and active role in this book. Cindy Rich was invaluable with her critiques, comments, and suggestions early in the manuscript. Ron Elkayam raised important questions which inspired me and ultimately gave the book more depth. I want to thank my editor Teddy Kempster whose sound judgment balanced what I wanted to say and how I should say it. I also want to thank Patricia Heinicke, Jr, L. B. Raid and Natalie Weinstein for their help with editing in different phases of the book. I want to thank David Kaim for his friendship and for the use of his computer when I really needed it. I especially want to thank Greenheart, not only for her encouragement and candor, but for inspiring me through example. She, more than anyone else I know, makes the world a better place.

Introduction

W hen I first heard a voice that said *Define God*, little did I dream that this was the beginning of a ten-year journey that not only would change my perception of God, but would also lead me to write a book. Whether the origin of the voice is otherworldly or comes from my own imagination is not what is important. What is important is that I, as a person who does not consider himself deeply religious or spiritual, felt compelled to try to define God. At first I was hesitant. How does one define God? I asked myself, Is defining God even possible? And besides, who am I to declare what is and isn't God? I wavered back and forth about the idea. I wondered if my audacity bordered on arrogance. I eventually got over my reluctance by surmising that if I undertook the endeavor with the right intention and motivation, then God should not have a problem with this spiritual and intellectual exercise. And besides, wouldn't God appreciate that I am reaching out, albeit in my own unique way?

I jotted down my first thought, spelling God not with a capital G, but with a lower case g. There was no issue about it, and it felt very natural to me. The Creator of the universe, I thought to myself, must be beyond having an ego and therefore probably would not quibble with such a minor detail. I continued jotting down definitions and before I knew it, I had a collection of meditations that differed from each other in approaches and belief, yet had common threads weaving them together. One such thread was that God had no gender. The second was that none of the meditations hinted that God had any inclination or power to hurt or harm in any way. The third was that the meditations did not seem attached to any time, place, or history.

Although I now had a number of definitions, I still had more questions, some of which that had been tugging at me for years: What is the purpose of God? What does God, as a truly enlightened and compassionate being, *really* want from humanity? And whatever God is, shouldn't God be a reflection of what is best in humanity, human thinking, and human consciousness?

It was then that I realized that God had evolved into god.

In that moment, I saw God in a different light. With a sense of excitement I re-read the meditations, realizing that I had before me an interpretation of God beyond anything I had ever heard or read about. I had somehow stumbled upon the simplest way to symbolize that god and the idea of god had evolved beyond ego, gender, and the need to judge, punish, or cause harm. I could not think of a more powerful way to show that god was now free from previous religious and historical associations. It felt revolutionary to me.

To my delight, another question soon followed: How can god be used as a catalyst or tool to heal the earth and to create a better world for humanity? This question was soon answered by more meditations, which underscored the notion that the power of god, rather than existing as a possible source of fear, could now be understood as an ever-present and accessible energy that empowers humanity to enrich life and increase goodness. With these new meditations came the awareness that not only can god grow as a symbol of what is truly good, just, and beautiful, but that through humanity god can be used to heal the earth and to create a better world. More significant, however, is that the ultimate power of god is in the hands of human beings, and the growth of god is actually dependent on humanity. I have found that the idea that *I* can and need to make god grow has transformed the way I look at life and the way I approach spirituality.

Although initially I had hoped to find a simple path of spirituality, the subject of God/god naturally lends itself to complexity. Each meditation in this book is its own way of relating to god, sometimes connected to other meditations and sometimes unique to itself. Like traditional God-based beliefs, there are contradictions in definition, understanding, and approaches to god, most of which are probably logically impossible to reconcile. Yet these contradictions, which include abstract and anthropomorphic notions of god, agnostic and declarative statements on god's existence, and the interplay of god as creation, god as creator, and god as created, are all purposely included for the sake of maintaining as many diverse spiritual perspectives as possible. Since the crux of this particular path stresses behavior rather than belief, contradictions as well as questions and doubts should not subtract from the two important elements that bind all the varied meditations: the benevolence of god in all its forms without the power to cause harm to anybody or anything, and the stress on goodness as a way to reach god and make god grow.

While the order of the meditations is intentionally sequenced, there is no correct way or order to read this book. Nor is there any expectation that every meditation will speak to everyone. If a single meditation speaks to the heart of a reader, then I will feel that I have succeeded. As a person who truly believes that spiritual diversity enriches humanity, in no way do I want to communicate that this or any interpretation is the correct understanding of God. I merely hope to reach out to those who, like myself, want to believe in God but for whatever reason may have found it uncomfortable, intellectually challenging, or morally questionable. I also hope that the word *god* can increasingly become synonymous with a belief system that is life- and earth-centered, stresses behavior over belief, and serves as an unwavering symbol for peace, non-violence, goodness, and religious tolerance. In its own small way I especially hope that god can serve as a catalyst for helping to create a better world.

B.H.

Berkeley, 2000

god

*G*od is being
and non being

god is creation, life,
and evolution

god is consciousness,
goodness, and joy

god is many
god is one

few things encompass
such infinite diversity

god can
and god does

god is complex and paradoxical
there are multiple ways
of understanding god

the more one understands god
the more of god
there is to understand

god grows.

New Beginning

*I*n the beginning
God commanded creation, the universe,
and the world of human beings

God acted as parent
for humanity in its youth

God guided humanity
expressing what was right and wrong

God demanded worship, faith, and obedience
God sat in judgment

God rewarded
and God punished

then one day
a human asked a question:
Does the power of God to reward and punish
make humans better humans
and improve the planet
for God's other creatures and creations?

the human
further pondered the nature of God
and then asked God:
What do You
as a truly enlightened
Being, Creator, and Life Force
really want from humanity?

God did not answer.

*W*hen the human asked God
what God really wanted from humanity
God did not answer
so the seeker continued to question

The human asked:
Does God really want obedience
and for human to have fear?

Does God really get angry?
Does God really punish?
If God is so great, would God have an ego?

then the seeker asked God:
Aren't gods reflections
of human beings' unconscious
and subconscious projections?

and god said
yes
they can be

then the seeker realized
that God should be a reflection
of what is best in humanity, human thinking,
and human consciousness

and then
suddenly and subtly

God evolved into god

and it was good.

*W*hen God evolved into god
the seeker knew
that this was a new beginning
and a new understanding
of the origin of life,
existence, and consciousness

god had suddenly evolved
from the need to judge, to punish,
and to hurt or harm in any way
to a state of pure goodness,
love, and peace

the seeker finally felt safe and secure
in the understanding
that god could never be used
as a reason or justification
to harm or threaten
any human, any life form, or the earth
for any reason whatsoever

the seeker smiled
knowing that god and humanity
were now both free
and sensed the limitlessness
of the unencumbered goodness and love
of god.

W hen the seeker contemplated
that god demands nothing
and that god is completely harmless
the seeker felt grateful and gratified
that there was no longer anything to fear
from the creator of the universe

the human also realized
that belief in god out of fear or guilt
or for purposes of power and control
is not only misguided but impossible
and that belief in god
without compassion and loving kindness
is meaningless and empty
like an unfulfilled promise

the seeker wondered
that if belief is not essential
what then is important to god?

so the seeker asked god:
What do you
as a truly enlightened being, creator, and life force
want from humanity?

and somehow
because god had evolved
from the need
for obedience, worship, ego, and power
the answer seemed more simple

the seeker realized that for god
belief in god is not as important
as how humans treat other humans,
other life forms, and the earth.

𝒰pon discovering
that god had evolved
beyond the need for power
and beyond the need to control human beings
the human asked:
What then is the power of god?

the seeker understood
that the infinite power of god
is defined by goodness, creation, and love
and that humanity
with its capacity for consciousness
is an agent of creation
with the power to expand goodness on earth

the seeker also recognized
that the power of god
as the source and symbol
of creation, goodness, and life
gives each human reason and purpose
to create a better world
and that the purpose of humanity
is connected and linked with god and goodness

but when the human truly grasped
that the power of god
is in the hands of humanity
and that humanity has the power to expand god
the seeker felt joy, awe, and hope
because the seeker knew
in that moment
that god had only begun to grow.

 Evolution

*J*n the beginning
with the creation of the universe
the law of nature was established
long before earth
and humanity on earth

the law of nature
which governs all physical forces
is not propelled by any notion
of what is good and what is not good

the law of nature makes no choices
and does not punish

the law of nature merely is

in its relationship to life and life forms
the law of nature is arbitrary and random
with instinct as the main guide for all life

humanity is conscious

human instinct can reflect
more than mere personal survival

human instinct can reflect
the wide range and realm of human consciousness

humanity can believe
that ego, selfishness, greed
and the need to exercise and accumulate power
are instinct
or that goodness, love, and the human spirit
are the true measure
of human life and human survival.

*T*he ability to feel pain
is a natural evolutionary stimulus
with a purpose
of helping an organism to survive

pain can come from and be caused by
nature and the law of nature
or from the consequences
of one's own actions
and the actions of others

pain and suffering
sometimes come from simple misfortune
which can strike randomly
regardless of the goodness of the individual
affecting even the blameless and the innocent
for few things in life are absolutely certain

sometimes
lessons can be learned
from pain and suffering

sometimes
pain and suffering can transform people
making them stronger, wiser,
and more compassionate

each person
can choose how to react
to pain and to the suffering of others

each person has the ability
to derive wisdom and strength from pain.

○

Pain, suffering, and martyrdom
are not a path to god
nor is god as consciousness
the cause of pain and suffering
for although pain
comes from life and the origin of life
god cannot wish pain on anyone or anything
for any reason whatsoever

pain is often an indication
that something is amiss
possibly needing remedy

god is goodness and faith
which are evolutionary tools
to remedy and help overcome pain and suffering
for the sake
of helping individuals and humanity
survive and thrive.

$\mathcal{E}$vil exists
and is a major cause
of pain and suffering
to humanity, life forms, and the earth

evil is neither other worldly nor cosmic
but is simply a consequence
of the human ability to make choices

whether as a single action
a series of actions
or a system
evil is created and perpetuated by humanity
individually or collectively
actively or passively
from choices based on narrowness,
selfishness, ego, or greed
and from the need
to exercise and accumulate power

evil causes injustice, pain, and suffering
when it is not necessary
or when there are alternatives

evil is destructive and self-destructive
with consequences often unforeseen
sometimes ultimately affecting the perpetrator
but more often affecting the innocent

the effects of evil
can happen years or even decades away
and sometimes last for generations

evil may or may not
ultimately destroy humanity and earth
but unchecked
evil can cause
an enormous amount
of damage and suffering.

O

Because humans can make choices
the potential for evil exists in everyone
with the measure of evil
varying from person to person
and ranging
from those who cause
immeasurable pain and suffering
to those whose existence is a blessing
because of their compassion and commitment
to humanity, living beings, and the earth

the potential for evil exists in humanity
as a consequence of human evolution
yet evil and the need to grapple with evil
helped to create and foster
human consciousness at a higher level
pushing humanity to question with greater depth
the meaning of life and existence
increasing the purpose of goodness and love
and propelling humanity
to evolve spiritually and morally.

O

Although evil is a barrier to human evolution
the true measure
of human evolution and survival
is based on the ability of humanity
to overcome, dismantle, and dissolve barriers
to goodness, love, justice, and life

evil can never be justified or legitimized
yet because of the urgent need
for goodness to grow
responding to evil
can help goodness and god grow stronger.

$\mathcal{G}$oodness is a force
and a way of being
that clarifies the meaning of life
and the purpose of existence

goodness embodies compassion,
understanding, tolerance, benevolence,
giving, loving kindness, and unconditional love

goodness is a key
to the well-being of humanity and earth
fostering justice, peace, life on earth
and the life of earth

goodness is the manifestation
that a person can live and thrive
beyond ego and mere personal survival
and help god grow

goodness is a path to human evolution
with the potential of transforming humanity
beyond the limits of biology
to a higher state
of being, existence, and consciousness

when goodness
free from motive, desire, attachment, and dogma
becomes instinct for all humanity
humanity will evolve to a state
where there are no barriers
between what is humanity
and what is god.

$\mathcal{E}$volution has enabled humanity
to understand evil, goodness, life, and death
giving humanity reason and purpose
to question the meaning of existence
and to question how to live life

evolution has given humanity
the capacity
to understand not only goodness and god
but that god grows
through goodness and human consciousness

evolution has given humans
the ability to understand
that although the rewards and losses of life
can be arbitrary and random
goodness, faith, and god
give humans the strength
to overcome the pain and obstacles
inherent in life and in the law of nature

evolution has given humanity
the capability to evolve from ego and power
and to evolve morally and spiritually

evolution has given humans the ability
to make the choice to evolve
and to consciously evolve
in the direction of goodness

evolution has given humans
the capacity to understand
not only that god exists and evolves
but that the evolution of god
reflects the evolution of humanity.

*H*umanity evolves
god evolves
god evolves with humanity

consciousness created humanity
consciousness created god

humanity and god created each other
humanity and god sustain each other

humanity gives god power
god gives humanity power

god has no power
beyond the laws of nature
unless given the power

together
the power of god and humanity
is unlimited.

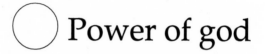 Power of god

*T*he power of god
which fills the world
with creation and existence
cannot be possessed or contained

god is true power

true power is beyond control
and the need to control

true power
is power that grows when shared

the true power of god
is life, goodness, giving, and love

through goodness and love
the true power of god
gives one
power beyond one's physical body
beyond physical life
and perpetuates existence
beyond one's life on earth

the true power of god
is a force
that when understood and used
spreads goodness, love, and life
increasing
one's power
the power of god
and the power of humanity.

*G*od is true power

true power is beyond control
and endeavoring to control
anybody or anything

as true power
free of ego
god is the power of creation
which does not determine nature
or acts of nature
for any reason whatsoever

as true power
god cannot harm, destroy, or control
nor can god
even want to harm, destroy, or control
rendering humans unable
for any reason
to harm, control, or kill
in the name of god

the power of god is infinite
the power of god is limited

the power of god
is a river of channeled energy and light
flowing more powerfully and directed
toward goodness, love, and life

within the limits of true power
through goodness, love, and giving
the energy of god expands infinitely.

*W*ithin the power of god
lies the law of nature
with consequences and repercussions
for every object and life form in the universe

within the power of god
also lies the law of goodness
with consequences and repercussions
for each and every human being

because humanity has the ability to make choices
humanity is beholden
to the law of nature
and to the law of goodness
which both lie within the true power of god
without the need or ability
for god to judge or punish

although some
may never feel the consequences
suffer for their choices
or even understand
that their suffering
ultimately comes from their own choices
there are consequences that sooner or later
cause pain and suffering
to others, life, and earth

although there are no guarantees in life
and good people sometimes suffer
there are also consequences
for fostering goodness
because goodness attracts goodness
and true power flows
towards those who foster goodness.

If one needs
a reason to foster goodness
it is not
because god consciously decides
to punish those who do not
but because the universe
rewards those who do foster goodness
sometimes in ways
that one may not foresee or know

if one needs reason to foster goodness
it is because the universe
often rewards in ways that are obvious and tangible
bringing into one's life
the magic of goodness
and the true power of god.

*E*arth is alive

earth existed
long before humans on earth

earth has the power
to live without humanity
and the power to sustain
humanity and consciousness

without earth
humanity has no power

without earth and human consciousness
god has no power

earth gives life to humanity
earth gives life to god

the power of earth is to sustain life

the better that earth
can sustain life and humanity
the more it increases
the power of god.

God is life
god is human consciousness

god has power
in life on earth
and in humanity on earth

as goodness and human consciousness
god has the power
to sustain earth and life

through human consciousness
the power of god
can help create a world
where there is harmony among humanity
and where humanity lives in balance
with earth and all of its species

with human goodness and consciousness
the power of god can create a world
where earth and humanity both thrive
making a fertile place
for god to grow.

 Human Power

$\mathcal{H}$umans are conscious
and have free will
humans have the power to make choices ·

the choices
that each human makes
though seemingly mundane and unimportant
affect the world more than one might think

there are choices
that damage life, humanity, and earth
and there are choices
that help sustain life, humanity, and earth

choices
based on narrowness, greed, ego, or power
or that threaten or endanger
humanity, life, and earth
not only create barriers to god
but limit humanity
and the growth of human consciousness
because the more
that life, consciousness, and goodness diminish
the more it decreases
the true power of every person
and the true power of life on earth

in the choice
of goodness, love, life, and consciousness
humanity is unlimited
because this is where one can find
god and true power

it is in the choice
of goodness, love, life, and consciousness
that not only
gives god purpose and helps god grow
but gives human beings
purpose and true power
to live, thrive, and evolve
as individuals and as a species.

*W*ith its myriad complexities
evil is the ultimate challenge to humanity

evil can seem daunting and overwhelming
not only in its size and scope
but in the inability of some
to understand
and appropriately respond to it.

Because evil is a consequence
of the human ability to make choices
humans have the responsibility of dealing with evil
by first understanding its complexities

some perpetuate evil for no logical purpose
or for reasons of power and greed
while others are motivated by fear and insecurity

some deny that their actions cause pain
while there are those
whose actions are motivated by pain

some close their eyes to the pain they cause
while others may not understand
the true consequences
that their actions have on others and the earth

evil has allies in silence and complicity
often in ordinary people
who may not be evil themselves
but who allow or perpetuate a situation or system
that causes pain
to human beings, life forms, or the earth

evil can never be excused or accommodated
yet the challenge of those struggling with evil
is to pursue justice rather than revenge
and to avoid judging others
especially those
who are vulnerable and motivated by fear

the challenge of those struggling with evil
is to show compassion with the understanding
that goodness and god is inside everyone.

O

The challenge of evil
is to maintain constant vigilance,
to constantly question,
and to keep one's eyes open

the challenge of evil
is to avoid using the struggle against evil
as an excuse
to control people
or to retain and expand power

the challenge of evil is to understand
that labeling people
and simplifying the struggle to good versus evil
can undermine goodness

the challenge of those struggling with evil
is to remain conscious
without falling into the delusion
of ego and self-righteousness
and to hold on to humanity and goodness
without absorbing the traits of evil themselves.

The challenge to humanity
is to learn from evil
and to acknowledge
that although evil is part of the human condition
humanity has the power
to make evil
an ever decreasing aspect
of humanity and life on earth

the challenge to humanity is
to become stronger from evil
to give strength to people
to turn away from fear and evil
and to help them
through genuine goodness
to decrease and ultimately desist
from actions that cause pain and suffering.

○

Humans have the power
not only to refrain from participating in evil
but to challenge evil
through awareness, involvement, goodness,
and compassion

every person has the power
to take steps
to shrink evil bit by bit
causing god and goodness to grow
giving more life
to humanity and earth.

*L*ove is the power
of giving and healing
love is the power
of healing humanity and earth

love is the power
that can make an enemy into a friend

love is the power
that gives humanity the ability
to nurture life and life on earth

love is true power
that cannot be contained
or taken away
love is power
that opens humans
to the energy of god

love is power that expands god

the more one loves
the more one spreads
god and god's love
helping god grow.

$\mathcal{T}$he simple power of goodness
is love and compassion in action

the power of goodness
expands god on earth
one act of goodness at a time

goodness is the power of god
accessible to everyone at any time

goodness is true power
that grows when shared
increasing power
both to the one who shares
and to the one with whom it is shared.

*T*he power of faith can create miracles

the power of faith can bring peace
between people and among nations

the power of faith can expand hope
in humanity, for humanity, and for a better world

the real power of faith is not blinding
nor does it narrow vision or fog reality

the real power of faith
cannot oppress anybody or anything
for without goodness, love, and truth
faith loses its power
and increasingly becomes an illusion

the real power of faith
exists in the realm of reality
and when engaged in meaningful action

the real power of faith
is a guiding beacon on the path of life
giving hope
and strength to overcome fear and despair
helping one see more clearly
in darkness and in light

faith is true power
that grows when shared

when faith increases love, goodness,
tolerance, compassion, and hope
faith strengthens humanity
and the power of god.

*A*n act of god
is benevolent creation

an act of god is giving

an act of god
by god or by a human
increases goodness, love, and life
for humanity and the earth

as creator or consciousness
god has given humans
the capacity to carry out acts of god
which include
giving and forgiving
struggling for justice
comforting the sick
healing humanity and the earth
nurturing and expanding peace
and any act
of compassion, goodness, and love

whether or not
god directly carries out acts of god
it is always within the power of a human
to carry out an act of god.

*H*umans are conscious

humans have the capacity
for creation and destruction
and the power to make choices

humans have the power
to live life consciously

humans have the power
to exist beyond mere personal survival
to consciously evolve
and to make the choice to evolve
individually and as a species

humans have the power
to understand and increase goodness

humans have the power
to give god purpose and power

humans have the power
to share
the true power of goodness and love
which increases the power of humanity
and makes god grow.

Finding god

$\mathcal{T}$here are many paths of god
with different ways and directions

both paths of being and paths of doing
connect humanity to the infinite source
of creation, goodness, and life

paths of doing
where there is a recipient
of goodness, love, and giving
not only bring the goodness of god
more quickly to others
but also reveal paths of god
so that others might see and travel their own path

the path of being
through equanimity, awareness, patience, and love
is a slower, more deliberate path
which not only can be more durable and steady
by helping one find god within
but can also lead to a path of goodness
and reveal other less-traveled paths of god

paths of god are paths to humanity and earth
making it easier
for humans to reach other humans
and for humans to connect with the earth

paths of god are paths to humanity
making it easier for god to reach humanity

the more one walks
a path of god and goodness
the likelier one is to encounter god.

*L*ove is a path of being
that can be simple, joyful,
and requires minimal effort

the path of love nourishes the soul
giving strength
to pursue other paths of god
making those paths more accessible, traveled,
easier, and more commonplace

love of life, for others, and oneself
is a path of god

love for all life
including humanity and earth
leads to opportunities
for traveling the path of goodness
which is the likeliest path
on which to encounter god.

*T*he path of goodness
can be a path traveled with ease
or it can be the biggest challenge in life

the path of goodness
is a path of doing and a path of action
with a recipient
of goodness, love, giving, and compassion

the path of goodness
requires more than just being
and sometimes more than merely behaving
for behaving without question or conscience
especially in an environment of injustice
can wither consciousness
and perpetuate suffering

the path of goodness
is more than not doing evil
for merely not doing evil
is nothing more than being neutral
going nowhere and in no direction

goodness
which is not always an easy path
is an active choice and a choice of action
needing open eyes and an open heart
sometimes demanding effort, causing discomfort,
and requiring more than merely behaving

goodness is a path requiring travel
which sometimes involves carrying others
and traveling through storms or even danger
yet within the path of goodness
lies the power of god and joy
which strengthens
and gives one energy to continue travelling

with each act
of goodness, kindness,
giving, and compassion
no matter how small
the path of goodness grows wider
carrying recipients of goodness toward god
and bringing god closer to humanity.

$\mathcal{G}$od is being
god is awareness of being

god is the awareness
of one's own existence
and one's own existence
in the universe

god is the awareness
of the existence and the being
of every other person
and every living thing

god is the connection
and the awareness of the connection
of all of life
and everything

stillness
and being without doing
increases awareness
making it easier
to listen
to one's heart and intuition
and to feel the presence of god.

*G*od expands
through goodness and love

god expands through giving

if there are questions
that each person should ask
they are:
What can I give?
What can I give to each person?
What can I give to humanity?
What can I give to the earth?

giving is expansion
giving is growth

giving is true power

giving without attachment
and without expectation of anything in return
expands god and oneself.

*G*ratitude is a path to god

gratitude increases awareness
of the gifts in life
helping one appreciate with awe
even the simplest gifts
that the universe has to offer

gratitude
for being and existence
especially for the simple gifts
encountered daily
even hourly
honors god and enriches life

the more
one acknowledges all the gifts
present in life and existence
the more one realizes
how many gifts there really are

acknowledging every gift
makes each gift significant
increasing its meaning
and the value of life

even if god
is not directly acknowledged
gratitude communicates appreciation
for what has been created
encouraging god and the universe
to continue creation
and to continue sending reasons
to be thankful.

$\mathcal{U}$nderstanding oneself,
others, and any situation
is a path of god
for god is reality
understanding reality
and existing in reality

the closer to reality
the closer to god

though the truth
can sometimes be relative, elusive,
complex, and even subjective
seeking knowledge, reality, and the truth
for the sake
of goodness, wisdom, justice, and understanding
and for reasons free of ego
increases the reality of god.

*N*on-judgment is freedom
to help god grow
free from the constraints and pitfalls of ego

non-judgment can help one avoid
a path of self-righteousness and hypocrisy
which increases neither one's power
nor the power of god

acting on one's beliefs
within a spirit of non-judgment
frees one from the burden of self-righteousness
increasing one's power overall
and in a given situation

living one's beliefs without judging
and with compassion and goodness
frees one's energies
for truly making a better world.

*G*od is beyond
human knowledge and perception

god is life, truth, and consciousness
god is the universe and infinity

god is greater
than anything that can hold an ego

seeking understanding
of consciousness, existence, and the universe
sometimes requires asking questions
of life, truth, and god

it is all right

it is all right
to seek god through questioning

it is all right to question god
and the existence of god

god should be questioned
it is only natural

as consciousness without ego
god welcomes and expects questioning

though some things are beyond answers
nothing in the universe
is beyond question.

*T*he purpose of god
is to create harmony
both in the mind and in the universe

the purpose of god is to grow
not through control or force
but through goodness and love

one way to help god grow
is through wisdom
which is the well
of goodness and compassion

one way to help god grow
is to learn wisdom
from all faiths and from all peoples
and to seek what one has in common
with everyone

how people drink from the well of wisdom
is not as important as what they drink
for spirituality and diversity of spirituality
only increase possibilities
to taste the sweetness of wisdom
and to access god

god's presence will be evident
when earth is a place
where wise humans and teachers
prophets and priests
holy women and holy men
of every nation, faith, and tribe
rejoice and celebrate
together.

*g*od is within
everything that lives

goodness and god are inside everyone

every encounter with every person
is an opportunity
to expand goodness and love

every encounter is an opportunity
to find and expand god
in that person
and within oneself

finding and acknowledging
god in everyone
even when it is difficult and challenging
helps god grow

god is love and life

it is through relationships
with life and humanity
that the relationship
between god and humanity
deepens.

God is in the moment

god is the infinite moment
with no beginning and no end

god is the moment in a spark of joy

god can be found everywhere
in each moment
and in every moment
of every living being

every encounter is an opportunity
to bring god into the moment
and to expand goodness and love

appreciating the moment
and what is in the moment
expands consciousness and enriches life

realizing and feeling god
in every moment
expands the presence of god on earth

welcoming god in each moment
connects existence to the infinite.

One can sense god
in the warmth of the morning sun

one can sense god
in the touch of a loved one

one can sense god in a taste that delights
one can sense god
in the presence of awesome creation

one can sense god
in music of beauty that touches the soul
and in the joy of dance
celebrating life and existence

one can sense god
in the fragrance of petals and
in the smell of leaves
whose roots
reach into the earth
and into the origin
of life and creation

god is sublime

one can feel god
in the awakening of the senses

one can sense god
in the awe and wonder
of being and feeling alive.

*G*od is everywhere

god is where god is apparent
god is where god is hidden

god is where god is
god is where god can be

god is everywhere
even in places
one might think are empty of god
for in those places
god also is
because
god can be
and god can grow

in those places
where god is not apparent
lie opportunities
to expand god
and to bring god into the moment

god is everywhere
god exists where god can grow

where god is the most hidden
is where god can grow the most

one can always find god
it just depends
on how and where one looks.

Benevolence

God is the energy
of infinite and perpetual creation
constantly sustaining
existence, the universe, life, and humanity

god created the world
to give the gifts of life,
to give existence a purpose,
and so that creation
would have its origin in goodness

god as conscious creator
creates goodness, love, joy,
and human consciousness
not only as ways to expand god
but also for their own sake
and for the benefit
of humanity and earth

god is the origin of being
and the consciousness
that created the world with a thought

god is the origin of goodness and joy
creating life and laughter.

*G*od is the essence of benevolence
which fills the world
with love and creation
and permeates existence
with life, goodness, and purpose

the essence of benevolence
is not to judge or harm
the essence of benevolence
is giving

god is benevolent
because god
cannot be anything but benevolent

god is benevolent
to inspire humanity
to aspire to greater goodness and love

when god and the image of god
are benevolent
people are more likely to reflect
the goodness and love of god.

*G*od is creation
god is benevolent creation

benevolent creation
for reasons of love, goodness, and giving
without control
and without attachment to outcome
is the origin of existence
because even though
god can control every thought, action, and moment
god does not want to control the entirety of creation
for if god determined the outcome of everything
not only would there would be no joy
in the mystery of creating
the universe, life, and human consciousness
but there would also be no real human creativity

the joy of benevolent creation
is not only to give the gift of life
but to give life freedom
to grow, evolve, and create

the joy of benevolent creation
is to encourage consciousness to grow
and to allow independent human creativity
in the hope
that humans choose goodness
which closes and expands the circle
of goodness, consciousness, life,
and god.

*T*he essence of god
is the infinite accessible energy of creation
which has given
every life form including humanity
the tools and abilities necessary
to conduct its life
free from external conscious intervention

while god can inspire and make its presence felt
it is not the nature of god
to overtly intervene
because for god to intervene
in a way that is obvious and discernible
not only can rob humanity
of the awe in the mystery of creation
but could also cause humanity
to become complacent and docile
by waiting for answers rather than creating answers
and to avoid responsibility instead of taking action

if god
were to overtly intervene in the affairs of humanity
it would hinder human evolution
and slow the growth of god
for the power of god grows
not through punishment, reward, and dependence
but through love and goodness for its own sake
with motives and intentions
free from fear, ego, control, and expectation

god is the essence of benevolence
which has given humanity
the freedom from intervention
and the power of free will.

*T*here is nothing to fear
from the essence of benevolence

there is nothing to fear from god

god creates
for the sake of giving

god does not create
for the opportunity
to judge, punish, and reward

god cannot judge, punish, or harm

god cannot want
to judge, punish, or harm

god cannot use fear and guilt
as tools for obedience

god has no need for obedience
god has no ego

god is the essence of benevolence
who creates from love
for the sake of love

god gives humans free will
so that they can choose goodness

more than anything
it is the human choice of goodness and love
that validates and reflects
the existence of god.

*S*ome can be close to god
without even knowing that god exists

one can be an atheist
and be very close to god

one can be a religious person
and indeed
be very far from god
for faith in god
without humility, compassion, or practicing peace
and without love for the earth, life, and humanity
is to be very far from god

god is benevolence beyond ego

god gives faith
not for the sake of god
but for the benefit of humanity
for god's benevolence
transcends any need
that god might ever have
for any human to believe in god

for god
faith and belief
in god and the existence of god
is less important
than hope, faith, and belief
in goodness, life, and humanity.

*G*od is with you
when you are born
and when you die

god is with you in trying times
and is also there with you
smiling at your joy

god is always with you
waiting to expand
ready to touch anyone
who calls
and who reaches out
through goodness, love, truth, and joy

whether or not
god has the power to change or move events
god is with you when you ride storms
and when you triumph
in your success of goodness and love.

*L*ove is the energy
that created the universe

love is the energy of god
making up the soul
of every living being

love is the energy
radiating from god
sustaining existence
and all life in the universe

god created the world
with love and for love

god created
the world and humanity
to expand love.

◯ Life

*T*he energy of life
flows through the universe
connecting every organism
with each other and to god

god is life
god is the universe
the universe is alive

god is the biggest organism
in the universe

everything that is alive
is a cell in the larger living body
of life

each cell is a cell of life

the body of the living universe
is god.

*G*od is the center
of creation and existence

the earth is the center
of life, human life,
and human consciousness

god is the universal life force
manifested and realized
through earth and life on earth.

The essence of earth
is to give and perpetuate life

the essence of humanity
is to live, grow, and evolve
on earth with earth
which is the source and center
of being, life, and human existence

the closer one is
to both humanity and the earth
the closer one is to god and to the center of life

the better that the earth
sustains life and humanity
the more it sustains the life of god.

*C*onsciousness beyond ego
is the realization and understanding
that all life is important
not only because humanity
depends on life and a healthy earth
but because other life
has value for its own sake

as part of life
human beings cannot live apart
from life on earth

as a species
humanity will succeed and evolve
by increasing human instinct
to encompass not only the life of humanity
but the life of the earth

humanity will succeed as a species
when human beings learn
that the purpose of life
is not to serve only humans
but that the purpose of human beings
is to serve and foster life
for both humanity and the earth.

*M*ost organisms
need other organisms to live
but no more than is necessary
to sustain their existence

one may have to kill to eat
but the more in harmony
with earth and with other organisms
the closer to god

god is consciousness
god is being conscious

the more that humans are conscious
of what they eat and consume
the more they sustain
consciousness and god.

Energy of god

The energy of god
flows through all of life
connecting every organism
in the universe

every organism
is a conduit of love and life
to and from god

god's love is magnified
through life on earth
through human beings, organisms,
and earth itself

each human is a conduit
that can expand the energy of god
by spreading goodness and love
to life on earth

the more
one loves and fosters
life, humanity, and the earth
the more that god
and the energy of god grow

acting as a conduit of god
makes one's energy
and the life of god grow.

 Universe

$\mathcal{G}$od is
the oneness and the infinity
of the universe and existence

god is a universe
god is the universe

god is the universe of consciousness
spanning
the human mind and the cosmos

every galaxy, star, moon, and planet
is a universe

each and every life form is a universe

the experience of life
for every living being
is a universe

humanity is a universe
each individual is a universe

the mind and each human mind
are a universe and a path to the universe

together
human consciousness and human evolution
can be an infinite universe
expanding the origin
of creation and goodness

everything is a universe
everything is the universe

life and consciousness are the universe
a different facet, a different view,
a different perspective,
a different understanding
of the infinite one and oneness
that is god.

*g*od is big

god is the biggest organism
in the universe

god is the universe

the universe is a cell of god
the universe is merely an atom of god

god is an organism
god is an organism of life flowing

every organism is part of god
with all of life connected

every organism is a cell of god

every cell in every organism is a cell of life
every cell is a cell of god

god is in every molecule
and in every atom making up every molecule

god is in everything
god is everything

every component
of every component
living and non-living
is god

god is small.

*G*od is the creation of the universe
and the universe of creation
which is the energy and motion
of goodness and god expanding

humanity is a creation of the universe
and a universe of consciousness
with the ability to perpetuate creation
and to expand the universe
beyond the physical world and biological life
into the realm of the spirit
by fostering goodness, consciousness,
and life on earth

god is creation
and the universality
of everything

god is creation
growing
though physical expansion
and through life, consciousness,
and goodness.

God is creation
god is being

god is everything

god is everything that is
and everything that is not

god is immanent
god is transcendent

god is the creator and the created
god is the path and the destination

god is everything that is not alive
and everything that is

god is everything that has ever lived
and anything
that will ever live

god is life
god is life beyond life

god is existence
and non-existence

god is the law of nature
and the force of goodness

god is every planet, star,
and galaxy

god is every atom, proton, neutron,
and quark

god is true understanding

god is the universe
and the human understanding
of the universe

god is evolution
god is faith

god is consciousness
god is oneness

god is earth
god is joy

god is the goodness
and the love that grow

god's components are infinite
god is one.

*G*od is one
god is oneness

god is unity among people
child, female, and male

god is the oneness of all peoples
of every color, heritage, and faith

god is the unity of humanity

god is the unity
of humanity and organisms
to foster life on earth

god is the oneness of the earth
with all of its organisms
living in balance

god is the unity of body and soul
god is the unity of heart and mind

god is the oneness of the earth and the universe
god is the oneness of the mind and the cosmos

god is the oneness of everything
god is being in oneness
with everything.

 Existence

$\mathcal{E}$very living being
has a purpose and a role

whether a person
realizes it or not
and even if that person
does not yet know what it is
everyone has a gift and a purpose
and a unique way
to express that gift and purpose

each person
has a unique way
that they can improve the world
whether it is helping a single human being
or struggling to sustain the earth
as a viable planet for all species

fulfilling one's purpose and role
in making the world a better place
empowers humanity
and helps god complete creation

fulfilling one's role
in increasing goodness
helps each person become a light among humanity

with enough lights among humanity
goodness and love will glow so brightly
that there will be no way
not to see and feel
the presence of god.

*A*s a conscious organism
each person is a carrier and messenger
of god's consciousness
and god's conscious presence

as conscious organisms
human beings have a purpose
in life
and as a species

the purpose of a human in life
is to find one's role in life
and to find goodness and god
within oneself
within every person
and within every living thing

the purpose of human beings
in life and as a species is
to expand goodness and love,
to help god grow,
and to nurture the earth
so that it sustains all species

the purpose of humanity as a species
is to consciously evolve
until there are no barriers
between humanity and god
for when humanity and god grow together
humanity and god grow into one

the purpose of humanity as a species
is to consciously evolve
until the consciousness of god and humanity
are one and one in the same.

*G*od has a purpose
god has many purposes

the purpose of god
is to increase harmony
in the mind and in the universe

the purpose of god
is to increase goodness, love,
tolerance, and peace

the purpose of god
is to benefit life and humanity
and to grow
through human consciousness and goodness

the purpose of god
is to give people faith in humanity
and hope for the future

the purpose of god
is to inspire people
to deepen relationships with others
and with the earth

the purpose of god
is to give humans the strength and ability
to overcome
the obstacles, difficulties, and pain
inherent in life

the purpose of god
is to give people
a sense of awe and wonder
about life and existence

the purpose of god
is to help humans cherish being alive

the purpose of god is to help humans
cherish human life, all life on earth,
and the life of the earth as the source
of being, consciousness, and god

the purpose of god
is to inspire and motivate
humans and humanity
to help earth nurture life for all species
and to create a better world for humanity.

○

Even if god is only an idea
god serves as a symbol and ideal
of what humans can aspire to

even if god is only an idea
the purpose of god is to create a world
where any god
reflecting the highest aspirations
of human goodness and love
could comfortably live and thrive.

*G*od is life
god is life beyond life

the universe and god
have not made apparent
the knowledge and understanding
of what comes after one's time on earth

if humanity had the capacity
to understand life beyond life
not only would life lack mystery and awe
but the knowledge
could overwhelm and distract humanity
from what is really important
which is life itself on this plane of existence
and living the best life possible
on earth with earth
with humanity, with goodness, and with love

the universe and god have not made apparent
the knowledge and understanding
of what comes after one's time on earth
because it is in the search for this knowledge
that one can find wisdom
and the true importance of life itself.

○

There is nothing to fear
from life beyond life
for life beyond life
is oneness with the universe, life, and god

life beyond life is true understanding
which is existence beyond ego
and the knowledge
of everything and the oneness of everything
including the universe, infinity, and god

life beyond life is existence
beyond the need for anything
or the need to understand anything.

○

Humans grow
by helping god grow

one certain way
to exist and grow beyond biological life
is to expand oneself while still alive
through goodness, giving, and love
to humanity and the earth.

*G*od is creation and life
god is everything

god is existence
and the infinity of the universe

god is beyond existence, space, and time
god is beyond perception and definition

god is a word

the word god is a symbol
for something beyond comprehension
for the word god
or any word or words
that try to label or describe god
is merely an attempt
to name and understand the great mystery
which is not only nameless
but is beyond language and human thought

god is a word
representing the true power
of infinite goodness and love
which grows
less though verbalizing and moralizing
and more
through acts of goodness
and living one's belief in god.

*G*od is goodness
and the manifestation and growth
of goodness

god is a way
of thinking, being, and acting

god is a way
of relating to life,
to the universe, and to humanity

whether god
created the universe
or was created by humanity
does not matter

what really matters
is how one lives life

what really matters
is if one increases goodness and love
and if one nurtures the earth
so that the earth sustains all life.

About the Author

Ben HaYim has worked in the fields of environmental planning, environmental activism, and education. Born and reared in the southwest United States, Ben HaYim now makes his home in northern California. This is his first book.

Order Form

Telephone orders (toll free): 1-800-431-1579
Online orders: www.ParenthesisPress.com
FAX orders: 510-883-9234

For Fax or Postal orders, please fill out and use this form.

Postal Orders: Please make check out to Parenthesis Press
and send to **Parenthesis Press Ordering**
        P.O. Box 2727
        Berkeley, CA 94702 USA

❏ Yes, I want ____ copies of *god: A Simple Book of Spirituality* at
US $12.00 each + $3.50 shipping (for up to 5 books via Priority
Mail). California residents please add $1.00 sales tax per book.

Payment:
❏ Check
❏ Credit card:
      ❏ VISA ❏ MasterCard ❏ AMEX ❏ Discover

Credit Card # _____

Expiration Date _____ / _____

Name on Card _____

Name _____

Address _____

City _____

State/Zip _____

Phone _____

Email Address _____